TRUMPET

101 MOVIE HITS

Available for
FLUTE, CLARINET, ALTO SAX, TENOR SAX, TRUMPET,
HORN, TROMBONE, VIOLIN, VIOLA, CELLO

ISBN 978-1-4950-6067-0

HAL•LEONARD®
CORPORATION
7777 W. BLUEMOUND RD. P.O. BOX 13819 MILWAUKEE, WI 53213

Visit Hal Leonard Online at
www.halleonard.com

CONTENTS

AGAINST ALL ODDS
(Take a Look at Me Now)
from AGAINST ALL ODDS

TRUMPET

Words and Music by
PHIL COLLINS

Moderately slow

ALFIE

Theme from the Paramount Picture ALFIE

TRUMPET

Words by HAL DAVID
Music by BURT BACHARACH

AXEL F
Theme from the Paramount Motion Picture BEVERLY HILLS COP

TRUMPET

By HAROLD FALTERMEYER

BABY ELEPHANT WALK
from the Paramount Picture HATARI!

TRUMPET

By HENRY MANCINI

BEAUTY AND THE BEAST

from Walt Disney's BEAUTY AND THE BEAST

TRUMPET

Music by ALAN MENKEN
Lyrics by HOWARD ASHMAN

BLAZE OF GLORY

featured in the film YOUNG GUNS II

TRUMPET

Words and Music by
JON BON JOVI

BLUE VELVET

featured in the Motion Picture BLUE VELVET

TRUMPET

Words and Music by BERNIE WAYNE
and LEE MORRIS

BORN FREE

from the Columbia Pictures' Release BORN FREE

TRUMPET

Words by DON BLACK
Music by JOHN BARRY

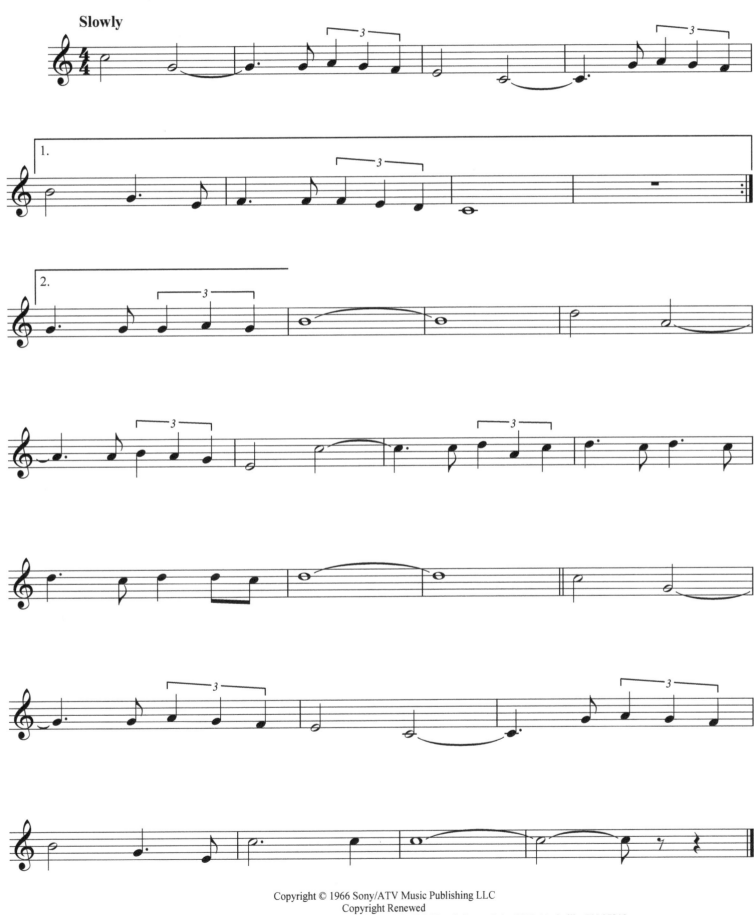

CALL ME
from the Paramount Motion Picture AMERICAN GIGOLO

TRUMPET

Words by DEBORAH HARRY
Music by GIORGIO MORODER

CAN YOU FEEL THE LOVE TONIGHT

from Walt Disney Pictures' THE LION KING

TRUMPET

Music by ELTON JOHN
Lyrics by TIM RICE

Pop Ballad

CAN'T HELP FALLING IN LOVE

from the Paramount Picture BLUE HAWAII

TRUMPET

Words and Music by GEORGE DAVID WEISS,
HUGO PERETTI and LUIGI CREATORE

Moderately slow

THE CANDY MAN

from WILLY WONKA AND THE CHOCOLATE FACTORY

TRUMPET

Words and Music by LESLIE BRICUSSE
and ANTHONY NEWLEY

CHARIOTS OF FIRE
from CHARIOTS OF FIRE

By VANGELIS

TRUMPET

Moderately, majestically

COLORS OF THE WIND

from Walt Disney's POCAHONTAS

TRUMPET

Music by ALAN MENKEN
Lyrics by STEPHEN SCHWARTZ

D.S. al Coda

CODA

COME SATURDAY MORNING
(Saturday Morning)
from the Paramount Picture THE STERILE CUCKOO

TRUMPET

Words by DORY PREVIN
Music by FRED KARLIN

CUPS
(When I'm Gone)
from the Motion Picture Soundtrack PITCH PERFECT

TRUMPET

Words and Music by A.P. CARTER,
LUISA GERSTEIN and HELOISE TUNSTALL-BEHRENS

COME WHAT MAY

from the Motion Picture MOULIN ROUGE

TRUMPET

Words and Music by
DAVID BAERWALD

DANGER ZONE
from the Motion Picture TOP GUN

TRUMPET

Words and Music by GIORGIO MORODER
and TOM WHITLOCK

DEAR HEART
from DEAR HEART

TRUMPET

Music by HENRY MANCINI
Words by JAY LIVINGSTON and RAY EVANS

DIAMONDS ARE A GIRL'S BEST FRIEND

from GENTLEMEN PREFER BLONDES

Words by LEO ROBIN
Music by JULE STYNE

TRUMPET

DO YOU KNOW WHERE YOU'RE GOING TO?

Theme from MAHOGANY

TRUMPET

Words by GERRY GOFFIN
Music by MICHAEL MASSER

DON'T YOU (FORGET ABOUT ME)

from the Universal Picture THE BREAKFAST CLUB

TRUMPET

Words and Music by KEITH FORSEY
and STEVE SCHIFF

THE DREAME
from the film SENSE AND SENSIBILITY

TRUMPET

By PATRICK DOYLE

END OF THE ROAD

from the Paramount Motion Picture BOOMERANG

TRUMPET

Words and Music by BABYFACE,
L.A. REID and DARYL SIMMONS

ENDLESS LOVE
from ENDLESS LOVE

TRUMPET

Words and Music by
LIONEL RICHIE

EVERYBODY'S TALKIN'
(Echoes)
from MIDNIGHT COWBOY

TRUMPET

Words and Music by
FRED NEIL

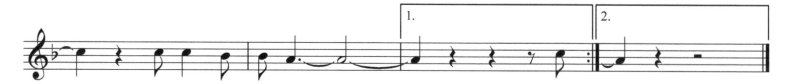

EXHALE
(Shoop Shoop)
from WAITING TO EXHALE

Words and Music by
BABYFACE

TRUMPET

Easy R&B Ballad

EYE OF THE TIGER
Theme from ROCKY III

TRUMPET

Words and Music by FRANK SULLIVAN
and JIM PETERIK

FOOTLOOSE

Theme from the Paramount Motion Picture FOOTLOOSE

TRUMPET

Words by DEAN PITCHFORD
Music by KENNY LOGGINS

FORREST GUMP – MAIN TITLE
(Feather Theme)
from the Paramount Motion Picture FORREST GUMP

TRUMPET

Music by ALAN SILVESTRI

HALLELUJAH
featured in the DreamWorks Motion Picture SHREK

TRUMPET

Words and Music by
LEONARD COHEN

GLORY OF LOVE
Theme from KARATE KID PART II

TRUMPET

Words and Music by DAVID FOSTER,
PETER CETERA and DIANE NINI

HAPPY

from DESPICABLE ME 2

TRUMPET

Words and Music by
PHARRELL WILLIAMS

Moderately fast

THE HEAT IS ON
from the Paramount Motion Picture BEVERLY HILLS COP

Words by KEITH FORSEY
Music by HAROLD FALTERMEYER

TRUMPET

Moderately fast Rock

HELLO AGAIN
from the Motion Picture THE JAZZ SINGER

TRUMPET

Words by NEIL DIAMOND
Music by NEIL DIAMOND
and ALAN LINDGREN

HOW DEEP IS YOUR LOVE
from the Motion Picture SATURDAY NIGHT FEVER

TRUMPET

Words and Music by BARRY GIBB,
ROBIN GIBB and MAURICE GIBB

I AM A MAN OF CONSTANT SORROW

featured in O BROTHER, WHERE ART THOU?

TRUMPET

Words and Music by
CARTER STANLEY

Moderately, in 2

I BELIEVE I CAN FLY
from SPACE JAM

TRUMPET

Words and Music by
ROBERT KELLY

I JUST CALLED TO SAY I LOVE YOU

featured in THE WOMAN IN RED

TRUMPET

Words and Music by
STEVIE WONDER

Moderately

I WILL ALWAYS LOVE YOU
featured in THE BODYGUARD

TRUMPET

Words and Music by
DOLLY PARTON

Moderately slow

small notes optional

I WILL WAIT FOR YOU
from *THE UMBRELLAS OF CHERBOURG*

TRUMPET

Music by MICHEL LEGRAND
Original French Text by JACQUES DEMY
English Words by NORMAN GIMBEL

(I'VE HAD) THE TIME OF MY LIFE

from DIRTY DANCING

TRUMPET

Words and Music by FRANKE PREVITE,
JOHN DeNICOLA and DONALD MARKOWITZ

JAILHOUSE ROCK

from JAILHOUSE ROCK

TRUMPET

Words and Music by JERRY LEIBER
and MIKE STOLLER

THE JOHN DUNBAR THEME
from DANCES WITH WOLVES

TRUMPET

By JOHN BARRY

KOKOMO

from the Motion Picture COCKTAIL

TRUMPET

Words and Music by JOHN PHILLIPS,
TERRY MELCHER, MIKE LOVE,
and SCOTT McKENZIE

Moderately bright

LET THE RIVER RUN

Theme from the Motion Picture WORKING GIRL

TRUMPET

Words and Music by
CARLY SIMON

LET IT GO

from Disney's Animated Feature FROZEN

TRUMPET

Music and Lyrics by KRISTEN ANDERSON-LOPEZ
and ROBERT LOPEZ

Slowly, in 2

Fine

D.S. al Fine

LIVE AND LET DIE

from LIVE AND LET DIE

TRUMPET

Words and Music by PAUL McCARTNEY
and LINDA McCARTNEY

Slowly

THE LOOK OF LOVE

from CASINO ROYALE

TRUMPET

Words by HAL DAVID
Music by BURT BACHARACH

LUCK BE A LADY

from GUYS AND DOLLS

TRUMPET

By FRANK LOESSER

A MAN AND A WOMAN
(Un homme et une femme)
from A MAN AND A WOMAN

Original Words by PIERRE BAROUH
English Words by JERRY KELLER
Music by FRANCIS LAI

TRUMPET

MANIAC
from the Paramount Picture FLASHDANCE

TRUMPET

Words and Music by MICHAEL SEMBELLO
and DENNIS MATKOSKY

Moderately fast

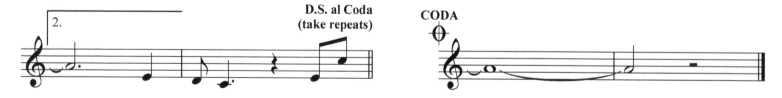

MISSION: IMPOSSIBLE THEME

from the Paramount Motion Picture MISSION: IMPOSSIBLE

TRUMPET

By LALO SCHIFRIN

MRS. ROBINSON
from THE GRADUATE

TRUMPET

Words and Music by
PAUL SIMON

MOON RIVER

from the Paramount Picture BREAKFAST AT TIFFANY'S

Words by JOHNNY MERCER
Music by HENRY MANCINI

TRUMPET

MORE
(Ti guarderò nel cuore)
from the film MONDO CANE

TRUMPET

Music by NINO OLIVIERO and RIZ ORTOLANI
Italian Lyrics by MARCELLO CIORCIOLINI
English Lyrics by NORMAN NEWELL

Moderately, in 2

THE MUSIC OF GOODBYE
from OUT OF AFRICA

TRUMPET

Words and Music by JOHN BARRY,
ALAN BERGMAN and MARILYN BERGMAN

MY HEART WILL GO ON

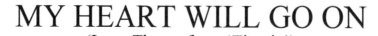

(Love Theme from 'Titanic')

from the Paramount and Twentieth Century Fox Motion Picture TITANIC

TRUMPET

Music by JAMES HORNER
Lyric by WILL JENNINGS

NINE TO FIVE

from NINE TO FIVE

Words and Music by
DOLLY PARTON

TRUMPET

NOTHING'S GONNA STOP US NOW

featured in MANNEQUIN

TRUMPET

Words and Music by DIANE WARREN
and ALBERT HAMMOND

Moderate Rock

OLD TIME ROCK & ROLL

featured in RISKY BUSINESS

TRUMPET

Words and Music by GEORGE JACKSON
and THOMAS E. JONES III

THE PINK PANTHER

from THE PINK PANTHER

TRUMPET

By HENRY MANCINI

PUT YOUR DREAMS AWAY (FOR ANOTHER DAY)

featured in INSIDE MOVES

TRUMPET

Words by RUTH LOWE
Music by STEPHAN WEISS
and PAUL MANN

PUTTIN' ON THE RITZ

from the Motion Picture PUTTIN' ON THE RITZ

Words and Music by
IRVING BERLIN

TRUMPET

Moderately, in 2

QUE SERA, SERA
(Whatever Will Be, Will Be)
from THE MAN WHO KNEW TOO MUCH

TRUMPET

Words and Music by JAY LIVINGSTON
and RAYMOND B. EVANS

Moderately bright

THE RAINBOW CONNECTION
from THE MUPPET MOVIE

TRUMPET

Words and Music by PAUL WILLIAMS
and KENNETH L. ASCHER

RAINDROPS KEEP FALLIN' ON MY HEAD
from BUTCH CASSIDY AND THE SUNDANCE KID

Lyrics by HAL DAVID
Music by BURT BACHARACH

TRUMPET

ROCK AROUND THE CLOCK

featured in the Motion Picture BLACKBOARD JUNGLE

TRUMPET

Words and Music by MAX C. FREEDMAN
and JIMMY DeKNIGHT

LOVE THEME FROM "ST. ELMO'S FIRE"

from the Motion Picture ST. ELMO'S FIRE

TRUMPET

Words and Music by
DAVID FOSTER

SAY YOU, SAY ME
from the Motion Picture WHITE NIGHTS

Words and Music by
LIONEL RICHIE

TRUMPET

SEPARATE LIVES
Love Theme from WHITE NIGHTS

TRUMPET

Words and Music by
STEPHEN BISHOP

Freely

THE SHADOW OF YOUR SMILE

Love Theme from THE SANDPIPER

TRUMPET

Music by JOHNNY MANDEL
Words by PAUL FRANCIS WEBSTER

Slowly, in 2

SOMEWHERE IN TIME

from SOMEWHERE IN TIME

TRUMPET

By JOHN BARRY

SKYFALL
from the Motion Picture SKYFALL

TRUMPET

Words and Music by ADELE ADKINS
and PAUL EPWORTH

SOMEWHERE, MY LOVE

Lara's Theme from DOCTOR ZHIVAGO

TRUMPET

Lyric by PAUL FRANCIS WEBSTER
Music by MAURICE JARRE

SOMEWHERE OUT THERE

from AN AMERICAN TAIL

TRUMPET

Music by BARRY MANN and JAMES HORNER
Lyric by CYNTHIA WEIL

THE SOUND OF MUSIC

from THE SOUND OF MUSIC

TRUMPET

Lyrics by OSCAR HAMMERSTEIN II
Music by RICHARD RODGERS

SPEAK SOFTLY, LOVE
(Love Theme)
from the Paramount Picture THE GODFATHER

Words by LARRY KUSIK
Music by NINO ROTA

TRUMPET

STAR TREK® THE MOTION PICTURE

Theme from the Paramount Picture STAR TREK: THE MOTION PICTURE

TRUMPET

Music by
JERRY GOLDSMITH

SUMMER NIGHTS

from GREASE

TRUMPET

Lyric and Music by WARREN CASEY
and JIM JACOBS

STAYIN' ALIVE

TRUMPET

Words and Music by BARRY GIBB,
ROBIN GIBB and MAURICE GIBB

THE SWEETHEART TREE

from THE GREAT RACE

TRUMPET

Words by JOHNNY MERCER
Music by HENRY MANCINI

SWINGING ON A STAR

from GOING MY WAY

Words by JOHNNY BURKE
Music by JIMMY VAN HEUSEN

TRUMPET

Bright Swing

TAKE MY BREATH AWAY

(Love Theme)

from the Paramount Picture TOP GUN

TRUMPET

Words and Music by GIORGIO MORODER
and TOM WHITLOCK

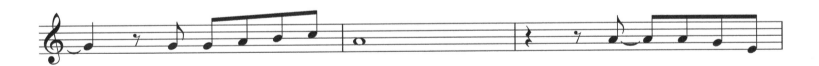

TAMMY

from TAMMY AND THE BACHELOR

TRUMPET

Words and Music by JAY LIVINGSTON
and RAY EVANS

THANKS FOR THE MEMORY

from the Paramount Picture BIG BROADCAST OF 1938

Words and Music by LEO ROBIN
and RALPH RAINGER

TRUMPET

THAT'S AMORÉ
(That's Love)
from the Paramount Picture THE CADDY

TRUMPET

Words by JACK BROOKS
Music by HARRY WARREN

A TIME FOR US
(Love Theme)
from the Paramount Picture ROMEO AND JULIET

TRUMPET

Words by LARRY KUSIK
and EDDIE SNYDER
Music by NINO ROTA

TIME WARP
from THE ROCKY HORROR PICTURE SHOW

TRUMPET

Words and Music by
RICHARD O'BRIEN

To Coda ⊕

Fine

D.S. al Coda

CODA
⊕

D.S.S. al Fine

TO SIR, WITH LOVE

from TO SIR, WITH LOVE

Words by DON BLACK
Music by MARC LONDON

TRUMPET

UNCHAINED MELODY

from the Motion Picture UNCHAINED

Lyric by HY ZARET
Music by ALEX NORTH

TRUMPET

TWO HEARTS

from BUSTER

TRUMPET

Words and Music by PHIL COLLINS
and LAMONT DOZIER

UP WHERE WE BELONG

from the Paramount Picture AN OFFICER AND A GENTLEMAN

TRUMPET

Words by WILL JENNINGS
Music by BUFFY SAINTE-MARIE and JACK NITZSCHE

THE WAY WE WERE
from the Motion Picture THE WAY WE WERE

TRUMPET

Words by ALAN and MARILYN BERGMAN
Music by MARVIN HAMLISCH

WHEN SHE LOVED ME

from Walt Disney Pictures' TOY STORY 2 - A Pixar Film

TRUMPET

Music and Lyrics by
RANDY NEWMAN

WHEN YOU BELIEVE
(From The Prince of Egypt)

from THE PRINCE OF EGYPT

TRUMPET

Words and Music by
STEPHEN SCHWARTZ

WHEN YOU WISH UPON A STAR

from Walt Disney's PINOCCHIO

TRUMPET

Words by NED WASHINGTON
Music by LEIGH HARLINE

WHERE DO I BEGIN

(Love Theme)

from the Paramount Picture LOVE STORY

Words by CARL SIGMAN
Music by FRANCIS LAI

TRUMPET

WRITING'S ON THE WALL

from the film SPECTRE

TRUMPET

Words and Music by SAM SMITH
and JAMES NAPIER

Slowly

YOU LIGHT UP MY LIFE

from YOU LIGHT UP MY LIFE

TRUMPET

Words and Music by
JOSEPH BROOKS

YOU MUST LOVE ME

from the Cinergi Motion Picture EVITA

Words by TIM RICE
Music by ANDREW LLOYD WEBBER

TRUMPET

101 SONGS

BIG COLLECTIONS OF FAVORITE SONGS ARRANGED FOR SOLO INSTRUMENTALISTS.

101 BROADWAY SONGS

00154199	Flute	$14.99
00154200	Clarinet	$14.99
00154201	Alto Sax	$14.99
00154202	Tenor Sax	$14.99
00154203	Trumpet	$14.99
00154204	Horn	$14.99
00154205	Trombone	$14.99
00154206	Violin	$14.99
00154207	Viola	$14.99
00154208	Cello	$14.99

101 HIT SONGS

00194561	Flute	$16.99
00197182	Clarinet	$16.99
00197183	Alto Sax	$16.99
00197184	Tenor Sax	$16.99
00197185	Trumpet	$16.99
00197186	Horn	$16.99
00197187	Trombone	$16.99
00197188	Violin	$16.99
00197189	Viola	$16.99
00197190	Cello	$16.99

101 CHRISTMAS SONGS

00278637	Flute	$14.99
00278638	Clarinet	$14.99
00278639	Alto Sax	$14.99
00278640	Tenor Sax	$14.99
00278641	Trumpet	$14.99
00278642	Horn	$14.99
00278643	Trombone	$14.99
00278644	Violin	$14.99
00278645	Viola	$14.99
00278646	Cello	$14.99

101 JAZZ SONGS

00146363	Flute	$14.99
00146364	Clarinet	$14.99
00146366	Alto Sax	$14.99
00146367	Tenor Sax	$14.99
00146368	Trumpet	$14.99
00146369	Horn	$14.99
00146370	Trombone	$14.99
00146371	Violin	$14.99
00146372	Viola	$14.99
00146373	Cello	$14.99

101 CLASSICAL THEMES

00155315	Flute	$14.99
00155317	Clarinet	$14.99
00155318	Alto Sax	$14.99
00155319	Tenor Sax	$14.99
00155320	Trumpet	$14.99
00155321	Horn	$14.99
00155322	Trombone	$14.99
00155323	Violin	$14.99
00155324	Viola	$14.99
00155325	Cello	$14.99

101 MOVIE HITS

00158087	Flute	$14.99
00158088	Clarinet	$14.99
00158089	Alto Sax	$14.99
00158090	Tenor Sax	$14.99
00158091	Trumpet	$14.99
00158092	Horn	$14.99
00158093	Trombone	$14.99
00158094	Violin	$14.99
00158095	Viola	$14.99
00158096	Cello	$14.99

101 DISNEY SONGS

00244104	Flute	$16.99
00244106	Clarinet	$16.99
00244107	Alto Sax	$16.99
00244108	Tenor Sax	$16.99
00244109	Trumpet	$16.99
00244112	Horn	$16.99
00244120	Trombone	$16.99
00244121	Violin	$16.99
00244125	Viola	$16.99
00244126	Cello	$16.99

101 POPULAR SONGS

00224722	Flute	$16.99
00224723	Clarinet	$16.99
00224724	Alto Sax	$16.99
00224725	Tenor Sax	$16.99
00224726	Trumpet	$16.99
00224727	Horn	$16.99
00224728	Trombone	$16.99
00224729	Violin	$16.99
00224730	Viola	$16.99
00224731	Cello	$16.99

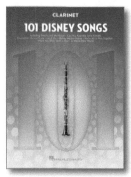

HAL•LEONARD®
www.halleonard.com

Prices, contents and availability subject to change without notice.